JOURNEY

THIS
JOURNAL BELONGS TO

Published by:
NIS VENTURES INTERNATIONAL
6391 Leisure Town Road, Vacaville, California 95687

Cover by Shelby Gibbs
Graphic Design Shelby Gibbs & Deborah Crone
Printed in The United States of America

WELCOME TO JOURNEY

Does God Dream? Scripture states that He never slumbers or sleeps. So, does he dream? I suggest He does. I would also propose that you and I are his dream. In Jeremiah 29:11 the prophet records God's own words: "I know the plans I have for you... plans to proper you and not harm you, plans to give you a hope and a future." In Psalms 39 David reflects on the number of thoughts that God has toward us in a day, and comes to the conclusion that they are good and innumerable.

One of the dreams God has for us is that we live in a hope anchored in everything He is. It is our desire to partner with God by offering this journal with inspirational hope thoughts to aid you in your journey.

The JOURNEY is your place to dream and hope with God. We have left the pages free of lines so you can doodle, sketch, write, and record your thoughts and imaginings. Our hope filled prayer for you is that the Lord make his face shine on you as you take this journey in the expectation of good.

-David and Deborah Crone

Quote Legend: *Prisoner of Hope*: From Prisoner of Hope, Captivated by the Expectation of Good by David Crone; *21 Days of Hope*: 21 Days of Hope, a Daily Encounter by David Crone; *Deborah Crone*: Deborah Crone

JOURNEY

When we choose hope, our whole being is aimed at abundance, promise, and destiny.

- Prisoner of Hope

JOURNEY

Hopeful living is being absolutely captivated by all the good God has prepared for us in this world and the next.

-21 Days of Hope

JOURNEY

I choose hope without apology and can honestly state that my experience in hope has left me without a competitive foe.

- Prisoner of Hope

JOURNEY

A pearl is evidence that beauty can outlast pain. Choosing
hope makes that a reality in my life.

–Deborah Crone

Choosing to be a prisoner of hope is to live with good as your expectation. and not the negative possibilities of your life situation.

-Prisoner of Hope

When we abound in hope, we are tapping into that which has an unlimited supply and superior quality.

Living in hope is to rest your future upon a God whose goodness is aimed at you.

-21 Days of Hope

In hope, I see what God has done and is doing instead of focusing on what the enemy is doing or what my circumstances are declaring.

-Prisoner of Hope

I can do more than I think I can if hope is my friend.

-Deborah Crone

We alone must decide to choose the option to be strong and courageous, to grab ahold of hope and refuse to release it.

-Prisoner of Hope

We have been invited by the Lord of Lords to experience a hope that can only be comprehended by those who respond to His invitation.

-21 Days of Hope

Hope is living above the facts and choosing the truth of
God's promises as our reality.

Never underestimate the power of a thought to feed your hope.

Hope erupts and is nurtured when we take what the scripture says about God, connect it with our personal history with Him and bring that into our present situation.

-Prisoner of Hope

Living In the house fear built defined my potential. Hope
helped me find the door into new territory.
                                                    –Deborah Crone

Hope is the enemy of hope's enemy. Sound like double talk? Then let me say it this way: Hope is the antidote to the hopelessness of delay.

-Prisoner of Hope

JOURNEY

Standing in hope turns the process of time from an enemy
to a friend and allows us an opportunity to cooperate with
the Holy Spirit and position ourselves to receive
the promise.

-Prisoner of Hope

Kindness is a powerful way to open the heart of a person and dispense hope.

-21 Days of Hope

———

Life around us is a blank canvas on which we can paint a picture of hope, using the brush of influence.

-Prisoner of Hope

Hope is a living, vibrant, and tangible force, moving us
from wishing to active expectation.

–Deborah Crone

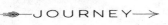

.

I am confident that a revelation of His goodness is the lens that allows us to live in hope.

-Prisoner of Hope

JOURNEY

We belong here, and if we are to live in full expectation of good, we must live boldly, not allowing fear to diminish our hope.

-Prisoner of Hope

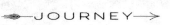

You are not a victim of your thoughts, but you have the power to choose the ones you allow to color your internal world.

-21 Days of Hope

Hope, anchored in Him, is guaranteed by His character and nature and empowered by the Holy Spirit who lives in us.

-21 Days of Hope

We cannot always determine our circumstances, and our history is what it is. But we can choose to live in hope.

JOURNEY

When we encourage someone to "take hope" we are handing them a tool that has the power to transform the way they see and live their life.

–Deborah Crone

The very nature of hope is made for the time of waiting—
for that time when what we hope for has not yet arrived.

-Prisoner of Hope

Hope has been such a powerful giver of life that no argument can persuade me to abandon it.

-Prisoner of Hope

His covenant promises to us are written with the blood of
his Son and stand true in the trustworthiness of
His character.

-21 Days of Hope

To accept that our situation is hopeless is to abandon our professed belief that God is greater than our circumstance.

-21 Days of hope

You can't reason your way into hope because hope at its very core is unreasonable. It must be chosen by an act of the will.

-21 Days of hope

Fear constructed a house around me that had no exits.
Hope built a door.

-Deborah Crone

Your thoughts have the power to either encourage hope or dampen your expectation. What you think about can be a hope-thief or a hope-expander.

-21 Days of Hope

Hope is established in truth that is believed and fully embraced.

-21 Days of Hope

Your hope is only as powerful as the one in whom you place your hope. Faithful is not just how God will always respond to you; it is who He is.

-21 Days of Hope

JOURNEY

Choosing hope enables me to leave behind those things
that would not benefit my future.

-Deborah Crone

The love of God guarantees that our hope placed in Him
will not leave us deceived or ashamed.

Choosing our perspective is imperative to keeping us living in hope.

When we recall His nature, the Holy Spirit increases our
revelation, and our hope levels accelerate.

-Prisoner of Hope

Hope allows us to believe, and therefore, move in faith
one more time, even when our history would
dictate otherwise.

-Prisoner of Hope

My present circumstances say, "give up". My destiny shouts, "choose hope".

–Deborah Crone

JOURNEY

Do the facts predict your failure? Well, this is your day to step over the facts and into the greater reality of God's promises by choosing to live in hope.

-21 Days of Hope

We have been called—invited—into a hope that can only
be fully understood when we see it through the eyes
of our inner man.

-Prisoner of Hope

Hope sees the invisible, feels the intangible, and achieves the impossible.

-Prisoner of Hope

Our hope is not just about us. When we choose hope, we inspire others to do the same.

I made the decision to live my life fully, despite my grief.
Hope made that choice possible.

-Deborah Crone

Choosing hope gives us the power to become the hero for our family, our society, and for generations we will never see.

-Deborah Crone

I am persuaded that hope, to be authentic, must be solidly anchored in something or someone that is trustworthy.

-Prisoner of Hope

Hope comforts us and helps us see that there is good in the midst and on the other side of our loss.

-Prisoner of Hope

JOURNEY

We've got God, and He's got us. It doesn't get any better than that.

—Prisoner of Hope

We can choose to be imprisoned by our situations, or be captivated by the expectation of good.

-Deborah Crone

Without hope, there is none.

-Prisoner of Hope

Living in hope requires tenacity, an unwillingness to let go
no matter how deep we are in the circumstances of life.

-Prisoner of Hope

Our hope will not abandon us because we are loved by the One whose love is deep enough to reach down to us in the time of our greatest failure or loss and restore us.

-Prisoner of Hope

When I began to focus on Him I am not only distracted from my grief, I am enveloped in His love and filled with fresh, effective hope.

Hope is not just sustained, but rather, it increases in potency when we recall the One to whom we really belong.

-21 Days of Hope

Unless we choose hope, activate our will, and go on a journey with the Holy Spirit, we will fail to gain the territory God offers us.

-21 Days of hope

Both His hope and His goodness are made for these times that we live in. They are specifically intended for seasons of hopelessness.

–Prisoner of Hope

Hope will hold us steady when circumstances give us reasons to run.

-Deborah Crone

Choosing to be a prisoner of hope is to rest your future
upon a God whose goodness is aimed at you.

-21 Days of Hope

My progress is not prisoner to my circumstance but my loss and failure are servants to my destiny.

-Prisoner of Hope

Hope is essential for sustaining faith, for it is the
expectation of good that feeds the level of
risk that faith requires.

-21 Days of Hope

The lens of God's goodness allows us to see through the
glare of the stuff of life and see the hope God
hides in every situation.

-Prisoner of Hope

Faith is the outworking of hope and the evidence that proves we have been living in hope.

-21 Days of Hope

When choosing Hope, joy comes in the mourning.

-Prisoner of Hope.

My destiny is waiting for me on the other side of hope.

-Deborah Crone

It is in the reality of God's presence that hope finds its authentication and substance.

-Prisoner of Hope

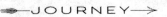

Hope does not live in the realm of, "What if...?" but in the atmosphere of, "Why not?"

-Prisoner of Hope

God's goodness and His hope shine brightest in the dark
times and prove their greatest strength in the
days of our weakness.

-21 Days of Hope

Living in hopeful desperation allows us to see beyond the cost and focus on the potential gain.

-Prisoner of Hope

When I choose hope, I give my heart and mind the command, as well as the permission, to search out hopeful things.

-Prisoner of Hope

I choose hope because I want my focus to be on the "above and beyond" that is my inheritance.

-Prisoner of Hope

JOURNEY

Hope stands in the face of everything negative and declares, "You will not defeat me." It prophesies into overwhelming circumstances, "This will not be the day of my setback."

-Prisoner of Hope

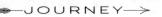

Hope keeps the door open to our destiny while closing
the door to the declarations of our circumstances.

-Prisoner of Hope

The quality of the lens will determine the accuracy of our perspective, and as prisoners of hope, we can choose the lens.

-21 Days of Hope

When we actively participate in prophetic words over our lives, they can then be used to fight off the forces of doubt and hopelessness. We can draw on their value and deposit them into our hope account.

-21 Days of Hope

Your thought life has the power to snatch expectation from the jaws of hope, or it can awaken hope in what seems to be a hopeless situation.

-21 Days of Hope

JOURNEY

As prisoners of hope, we leave our homes and enter the world with a confident expectation that shouts to all we come in contact with, "I'm a carrier of hope, and that hope is chasing you down!"

-21 Days of Hope

We will not be disappointed in hope because His love is high enough to draw us into heavenly realms so that we are seated in heavenly places with Christ.

-Prisoner of Hope

Expectation is the essence of hope. When we hope, we are setting our focus with confidence that we will receive, or see, that for which we are hoping.

-Prisoner of Hope

JOURNEY

Living in hope requires apprehending the promises and holding on for the long haul, seeing the journey through the lens of hope.

-Prisoner of Hope

HOPE TRILOGY NOW AVAILABLE

Books can be purchased at www.imissionchurch.com
or www.amazon.com

Made in the USA
Lexington, KY
22 September 2018